my wounds + yours

By
Addison Shafer

CONTENTS

My Wounds

Your Wounds

Authors note

these pages are heartbreakingly beautiful and this book was not easy to write. all that ask from you my reader is that you will be gentle with my story and if your story sounds anything like mine then you must know, it gets better. this pain is temporary and your wounds will heal, like mine.

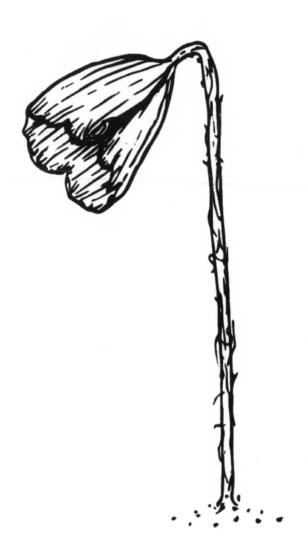

this book is for the healing, the healed,
and all who come in between

my wounds

No Mercy

Depression does not discriminate.
It doesn't care about your gender
or religion.
Depression isn't picky,
and it sure as hell isn't nice.

It doesn't want to get to know you,
because it doesn't care
what your last name is
or your favorite movie.

Or maybe
depression does want to know you.
Maybe it wants to get close to you
to know your secrets and fears.

But I know for sure it wants to destroy you,
and I know for sure you think it will.
At times, it seems too heavy
for your tiny shoulders to bear,
but look up, child.

I know for sure
you are strong enough to do this,
and I understand there are days
where getting out of bed
is a battle in itself
and your sheets wrap around you,
begging you, "please don't go".

But I also know
it gets better,
This is temporary.
This, I know

Today's Task

Loving myself is a task
I'm often not good at,
but loving myself
without someone else to love me
is nearly impossible.

The side effects of hurting

My stomach rumbles protesting today's skipped meals.
Shark week skipped two months.
I could knit a scarf out of the hair in my brush.
I eat tic-tacs until my tongue bleeds orange,
at least they are calorie free.
My throat burns from the throw up
and I've lost count of the napkins full of food I've thrown
away.

The side effects of healing

One burrito gives me the stomach of a women in her
first trimester.
I get bloated if I eat a full three meals.
After every bite I feel guilty for eating,
but I know starving myself is feeding my demons.
I watch my parents hesitate to ask if I've ate today
and see it kills them when I can't give a straight answer.

Winter Weather

You are like the snow:
beautiful chaos.

People anxiously wait for you,
but when you come, we'll get mad
if you aren't the perfect amount for us.

You can't be too little,
but you can't be too much.

With beauty, there always comes chaos.
Soon after snow, there is a mess:
trees snapping at the weight of the white,
roads slippery with the aftermath of ice.

In this world, I was taught to measure myself.
Every morning, I grab the scale and the mirror.

I rip out my ugly.
I weigh myself to make sure I'm just right.
Just right for you.

You can't be too big,
because then you'll be called fat,
but you can't be too skinny,
because then you're anorexic.

Don't be too emotional.
Then you're just dramatic.
But if you aren't compassionate enough,
you're just heartless.

I've mixed myself into a potion:
a dash of pretty
paired with some humble
along with determination.

As a little girl
growing up in a world
that tells you who you have to be,
it's hard to find out who you truly are,
but I know you are truly amazing.

Pills

Every time I take a pain killer,
I have to convince my body I'm not trying to kill it.
My throat tightens at the thought of swallowing a pill,
my jaw locks up when I catch a glimpse of the medicin
cabinet.
My stomach begs to let it back up, after I gulp it down.
I have to promise that it's okay.
My brain understands, but my body does not.
I hope my body begins to trust me again.

Merry Christmas

I've been treated like wrapping paper.
You cut me open.

Someone came along
and taped me back together
only for me to be torn apart.

Anxiety

Dear anxiety,
You cause me to overthink.
You send me into panic mode.
You make me have
constant first-date butterflies in my stomach,
and in fear of saying something wrong,
you've stitched my lips together like a quilt.

You silence me
with the lies you put in my head.
You plant them one by one
so my beautiful brain is overwhelmed
with the weeds you obsess over.

At my house,
in my bathroom,
when I look in the mirror,
ugly is imprinted on my forehead.

Dear anxiety,
You force me to overanalyze everything.
You make me break down the simplest task and make i
the hardest.
You've gotten me to the point
where I refuse to ask for help.
You convince me I'm a bother
and a problem.

Every time you creep up on me
like the moon does the sun,
my body shuts down.
I panic.

the panic manifests in my gut.
I feel you under my rib cage.
You've cracked open my chest,

and now I can barely breathe.

Dear anxiety,
I've heard you're close friends with depression.

Dear anxiety,
I'm sick and tired of you dictating what I can and cannot
do.

Remember that I know I'm fucking gorgeous
even when you scream that I'm ugly.
Remember that I know
the world won't come crashing down
if I ask for help.

So stop trying to sew my lips shut.
I refuse to be silenced.

Stop Dancing

These silly boys,
they think I don't know their motives,
but I know.
I watch as they dance around questions
and tiptoe around certain topics,
avoiding anything that might make them
feel some type of way.

Shame

Cutting means
long sleeves and jeans
even though its 90 degrees today.

Cutting means
no swimming this weekend
and having to tell Mom why.

Cutting breeds shame.
Learn to love your scars
but remember why
you don't make them anymore.

Band-Aid

Sorry doesn't cut it
when you've cut me so deep.
Your apology is meaningless
after you've spit such fiery words
at my self-esteem.

Working with Myself

I used to find it easier
to hide from my problems,
to ignore their very existence.
Maybe I'd shove my face in a book,
try to surround myself with people,
do anything in an effort
to distract myself from reality.
Some weekends, I spent in bed,
watching movies.
Perhaps taking three showers a day
would take all the hurt away.

But then I realized
no matter how much I scrubbed my body,
I would never feel clean.
No matter how many movies I crammed in,
it would still be impossible to ignore
the taunting thoughts.
No matter how many books
I managed to read,
no matter how much I socialized,
I would still feel the same loneliness and hurt.

And honestly, distracting myself worked
for a good while,
but I wasn't dealing with the hurt.
It was only manifesting in me.
Eventually, I grew out of hiding from my pain
and instead began to run.
Running and hiding are similar.
Maybe I was running in search
of finding somewhere else to hide.
Really, I'm not sure,
but I know neither running nor hiding
helped me heal.

Painful Poem

A boy in class joked, 3rd times the charm after I recovered from my 2nd suicide attempt.

On the bus a boy made a twisted comment, saying who is such a mistake that they can't even succeed in committing suicide.

A girl at lunch told me I wasn't really depressed and I tried to kill myself for attention.

In the middle of a panic attack, at school, a teacher yelled "what's wrong with you?"

Sweet aching soul, let the past suicide attempt be the last. Surviving an attempt is the world saying it needs you here. You are seen and what you feel is real, hurt people, hurt people.
There is nothing wrong with you, don't be ashamed of your anxiety, accept it.

Shower Thoughts

Have you ever been in a shower so hot
That it's almost hard to breathe?
Your throat is filled with steam
too thick to let air fill your lungs.
You can almost feel the heat in your chest,
kind of a burning, tingly sensation.
It's so steamy you have
to pull back the shower curtain
and catch your breath.

It's such a relief when the cool air
enters your mouth.
After a quick second of gasping,
you snatch the curtain and close it.
Five minutes later,
you will repeat these motions.

A hot, steamy shower
is a minor glimpse of what it feels like
for me to panic,
so when you are stuck in one,
clenching onto your shower curtain
for cool air,
I hope you think of me.

Little Boys

I won't lie.
When a boy tells me I'm pretty,
I no longer feel a feeling.
My cheeks don't turn rosy,
And butterflies don't flutter in my stomach,
because I've realized
it's just meaningless words
slipping from the lips of stupid, young boys.
My rosy cheeks have turned gray.
My face is now pale
from the sick sadness in my heart.
My butterflies were murdered
by the last boy to tell me I'm pretty.

Words no longer have purpose
because they are overused
and said out of context.

"I love you"
is now a laughable statement.
After I kiss a guy,
all of a sudden, he "loves me"
when all he really wants to do
is stick his hands up my skirt.

Fortune Teller

Her sweet smile had collected dust,
and her eyes no longer sparkled
like they once had.
She found herself in a constant state of loneliness.
It was so uncomfortable,
because it had become familiar.

This is a tragedy
because she is a girl
who finds comfort in knowing things.
If she had a choice,
she would wrap a multi-colored turban around her head,
hover her fingers over a crystal ball,
and transform into a fortune teller.
Maybe then she could look in the mirror
and see purpose,
see a plan,
see a future.

Generations

My generation walks on a bed of thrones.
We bear broken homes with absent fathers
and carry bandaged hearts
weighted by scars.
My generation looks depression in the face
and greets suicide with a smile
and a handshake
because it is nothing but familiar.
Half of the girls in my kindergarten class grew up
with the sad fate that hands would soon be
places unwanted and undeserved.

So tell me my generation has had it too easy.
Tell me we are lazy and privileged,
that we are self-absorbed
and don't know what hard work is.
Tell me that we are ruining religion
and are phone-addicted.
Tell me we are whiney, thoughtless, rude.

But you must remember
we are growing up in a world
that everyone is just now figuring out,
puzzled by technology and global warming.
We are facing issues
that never crossed your mind.

Rush + Roulette

Depression likes to play
a game that involves me
and a single round of bullets.
It's a lethal game,
dependent on luck,
with no mercy.
Either depression dies
or I do.
I'm determined to win.

Forgetting

Today the clouds set down on the mountains.
The fog-covered skies reminded me of you.
The white mist blanketed my small world
for a temporary work of art,
kind of like you,
like the way your body covered mine,
but only for a short time.

The bluish fog reminded me
of staring into your eyes,
but then I watched you disappear.
You left pieces of yourself behind
as a reminder,
like the little patches of fog
outside my window today.
You stuck around in my mind,
hard to erase,
but I promise I'll forget about you
and how easily you disappeared.

Come out + Play

Tonight the winds are roaring
and screaming at me, "Run!"
The crystal seas are churning,
and I'm begging for the sun.

This night, I'm extra lonely.
I'm pleading for someone,
you or someone like you,
really just anyone.

Preoccupied

I apologize if I ever seem preoccupied.
I promise it isn't you; it's me,
and I know you've heard it before.
I don't want to be a broken record
or tell you clichés.

You aren't the problem.
It's just recently I've lacked motivation,
and anytime I get away from everyone,
my mind wanders,
I'm tired of babysitting myself,
always keeping tabs on my mood.
At times, it's like nothing can make me happy.
I don't have much to look forward to
but you.

Procrastination

I have spent too many days
looking for a reason to stay,
searching for a purpose
and trying to shuffle through all my emotions.
They are thicker than a deck of cards.
I've spent hundreds of hours
doing my best to keep myself busy:

drowning in *Law and Order* reruns
and eating way too many snacks,
mostly salsa.
Busy is now just a distraction.
I'm procrastinating
on more than just a homework assignment.

Bold Blue

The sapphire-blue waves
crashed against the rocks,
creating a sound that shook my body
and drove out any thoughts of you.
The ocean would settle
before letting out its next roar.
I was in love with the view.
If only I could marry it.
It swore to be
much better to me than you.

Branded

My fist are clenched so tight,
like the straight jacket that held me all night.
Your hands like rubber gloves,
roughing up the inside of my thigh.
It took years until I could look myself in the mirror
and not see the mess you made of me.

Equal

What if I told you that you equal one pill,
that what you said equals two pills,
or that your absence was equivalent to four.
Everything you do
means something to someone.

On that really lonely night
when I consumed many more pills
than one or two or three,
did you care?
Did you take the time to think about me
about how you treated me or what you said
or how you left
You equal one pill.

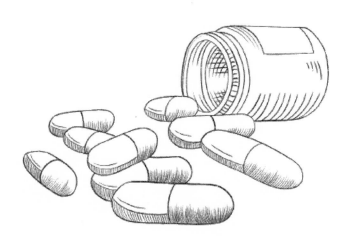

Let Me Be the One

I want to be the answer
to all your questions why,
but I get so wrapped up in the fact
that one day you might say goodbye.

Well Worth It

Today I am living for you
because I don't want to live for myself.
I'm waking up
determined to survive the day
because of your smile,
and I know if I leave,
I'll be taking that with me.
Many days, suicide dances in my head,
singing only sad songs
whose words I have now memorized,
but you are a reminder
that life is worth living.

Summers

I miss summers with you,
where my thighs would stick to your black leather seats
and trips to cookouts for milkshakes
was a daily thing.
I always got mint chocolate chip,
and you got some peanut butter concoction way too
sweet for me.
Most the time, you ended up drinking
half of my milkshake, anyway.
Turns out I'm extremely susceptible to
brain freeze.

Take me back to our late-night drives
when I couldn't sleep
or days on the river
that went by way too quick.
We soaked in that green chemical swamp all day,
without a care,
just you and I

I miss campfires
and listening to you play guitar until 1 am,
and I don't remember
if you liked your marshmallows burnt or toasted,
and for some odd reason, I am dying to remember.
Time and distance have caused me to forget a lot.
I don't just miss the summers;
I miss you.

Harper Kate

I am a lot like Harper Kate,
only she's a lot cuter, way more annoying,
and also a dog,
but besides that, we are very similar,
constantly craving attention
and very dependent on others,
only she can't help but be dependent,
and well, for me, it's just a bad habit.

Sometimes when she's trying to play, she hurts me,
and I may do the same to you
in my efforts to love you.
I cause you pain,
can I blame Harper Kate?

Body, Please

I'm trying to get my body to understand
what my brain can't get.
I am dying to eat,
but I can't stomach the thought of food.
Eating an almond is pushing the limit.
Body, please hang on.
A mix of self-hatred and depression
consumes my appetite.

I'm trying to give you what you need.
Can you forgive me
for all the skipped meals
and finger-gagging trips to the bathroom?
Body, please.

Teach Me How to Forget

My room reeks of loneliness,
and the air is stale with disappointment.
I'm talking to my ceiling fan
while I lie half-naked in bed,
trying my best to erase everything you said.

Mandala

If my life were a mandala,
a complex design of
swirls and awkward shapes
for my Creator to color,
I hope he would color me bright,
fill me with yellows and pretty pinks.
I hope he would steer away from dark shades
and focus in on my details.
A glimpse at my page may be overwhelming
and seem impossible to complete,
but it will be eye-catching.
Whether complete or unfinished,
I am a work of art.

Trigger warning

When you lay your hand on my thigh,
my brain sends a quiver down my body.
It tells me I should run.
The panic scratches it's way down my throat.
My heart beats quickens,
matching the pitter patter of a young girls feet
chasing after the ice cream truck.
I tell my brain it's okay not to flee,
this time you can trust me.

Buzz Bitch

One day, all the lies you screamed
will become mere whispers to me.
The thought of you won't roar like a lion
But will be so faint and small
that I can shoo it away like a bug.

Caution

After you left,
I bandaged my heart with caution tape
and began wishing on shooting stars,
not for your return,
but for all the memories of you to vanish.
I no longer wanted my heart to be
a museum of the souvenirs you left behind.
It has been months since you deserted me,
and still, you linger in my mind.

You reminded me that building
a drawbridge to my heart was necessary.
I don't want to keep people out,
but just be cautious about who I let in,
because you didn't deserve
to venture through.

Blame Game

Many things I just blamed you for.
You were an easy target.
Some of the blame, you much deserved,
but I cannot hide behind the pain you caused.
I can't use you as an excuse,
because it simply would be
trapping myself inside a cage,
and I am no victim.

Ashamed

When I say I have a stomachache,
I mean I'm really anxious,
but I'm too embarrassed
to say aloud
that I have anxiety,
so instead, I'll ask to go to the nurse,
when really I run to a bathroom,
lock myself in a stall, and cry
because my anxiety is screaming at me, "Run!"
and I feel trapped in my own body.

Mirror

Too many tears
shed in front of the mirror
that whispers to me
the lies of silly boys
with too much testosterone
and not enough common sense.

I stare into the eyes of a girl
who isn't too kind to herself.
I look at someone
I don't even recognize.

My eyes tell a story,
one you don't want to read before bed.
Looking closely enough,
you'll see the grief behind my smile
as I hold onto
the bittersweet memories of you,

Open House

You left my heart vacant,
and you must have forgotten
to put back the "For Rent" sign,
because no one has filled me up since.

I've become tired of my renters.
They never take good care of me,
because they are simply passing through.
I need someone to
paint over my scrapes and bruises.
hang pretty picture over the dents.
and remind me I am worth the work.

Divorce

Peering through the glass door,
hands gripping the knob already,
anxiously, I wait to see Daddy.
He is always running late,
but I'm just happy he decided to show up.

Multiple Christmases,
Every year brings the great debate
of deciding who to spend my birthday with.

In the end, both my parents
are missing 50% of my life,
50% of my memories.
One parent is going to miss my first break-up,
and the other my first date.

I get tired of dragging my blanket back and forth
and never having the shirt I want to wear
at the right house.

I hate asking Dad to buy my tampons,
and Mom doesn't like baseball.
There is no upside to divorce.

Smoke Break

You are my smoke break,
my breath of fresh air,
and you give me relief,
the same kind I get
when I wake up from a nightmare
and realize it is only that,
a nightmare.

Happy Father's Day

How do you write a Father's Day card
to a dad who's so distant,
to a dad who isn't in your day-to-day life.
I can't just fill it with cheesy shit like
"you're the best dad" or
"Thanks for always being there"

because you're not the best dad
and you're rarely there,
so maybe just something like
"Thanks for being my dad."
Honestly, sometimes that's the extent of our
relationship.
Sometimes you are nothing more
than a stranger
I call my father.

Glow

I love anything that glows in the dark,
and I consider myself
to be a glow-in-the-dark kind of girl,
but just like anything that glows in the dark,
occasionally, it runs out of light,
so you set it out to recharge.

On days where I don't want to get out of bed
and all my glow is gone,
drag me outside.
Take me to see the light.
Recharge me.
I was born to glow.

Coming Home

When I went home
for the first time in over a year,
everything was different.
Daddy, you had built walls and fixtures.
You'd painted
and moved around the furniture.

My room was being lived in
by another little girl.
Was she calling you daddy now, too?
And in your room, there was another woman.
I didn't even know her full name.
Did you?

I missed my home,
and I came back
to find out it didn't miss me.
It wasn't empty like I was.
You had filled it up
with more people, different people.
It no longer smelled the same.
I couldn't pick out the dusty scent
with hints of your cologne.
Maybe the other women didn't like the smell
or the color of the walls
or the arrangement of furniture,
and of course,
you're willing to change it all for them,
other women.

Morning moans

The flicker of my eyelashes echoed,
reminding me of just how alone I really was.
My bookshelf a collection of poetry,
telling me I still had work to do.
I roll over and my bed sheets scream "whore".
I couldn't bare looking in the mirror anymore.

He loves me, loves me not

Petals falling to the floor,
he said he doesn't want you anymore.
As the words slip from his lips,
your tears will drip right off your cheeks,
right down your neck, unto your sheets.

+ yours

This half is yours. I dedicate it to you. My vision for this section was to give a voice to every person I interviewed. There is power in sharing your story, I learned that from sharing my own.

Questions

1. What is something you regret?

2. As a child, what did you dream of being when you grew up?

3. What's something you're self-conscious about?

4. What has been the most influential experience in your life?

5. Five words to describe yourself.

Sabrina/Mom/37

The butterfly effect of bad decisions,
tangled her in a situation anyone
would struggle to navigate.
And the result of events
ended with an unborn baby.

Barbie houses adorned
in nothing but finessed décor,
she wanted to make a living
out of this very thing,
Design and decoration,
only math stood in the way,
or she would be on HGTV.

Shorts don't fill her drawers;
she likes long dresses.
That blanket over her legs,
she does her best to hide
her pale complexion,
which causes her to bruise like a peach.

Travels over the big pond
to a tiny country
filled with people she grew to love
shaped her in ways she never thought possible.

She describes herself as
tenacious, genuine, fearful,
contradictory, and sarcastic.
I can confirm the last one.

Steve/Stepfather/39

The combination of being young
and hurting resulted in bad decision being made.
Now he carries the regret of those mistakes,
something no one wants to live with.

He would grow to love
drumsticks in his hands.
A rock star is what he wanted to be.
He definitely had the looks for it,
long black hair, pierced ears and funky glasses.
(This look was pre marrying my mom)

Body image issues
that everybody has,
He has, too.
A little belly and not enough hair,
but I have known him no other way.

Being a son of God
and a follower of Jesus
has grown him into the person he is today.
Which is an amazing Father,
who would let me paint his nails.
Despite the fact he had to work that same day
and set through brutal tea parties,
when he could've been watching the game.

Introspective, creative,
musical, funny,
and curious, are words he used to describe himself.

He wears regret on his face.
Looking back, he's made many mistakes.
He should have put the ones he loved first.
But what do you do when the damage is done?
And the mistakes that you made are too big for an
"I'm sorry" to fix?

As a young boy, baseball was his passion.
Many days were spent on the field.
Summer was consumed with games.
He had dreams of the major league.
Proudly he wore number 10 on his back.

His face is full, with thick black hair.
I suppose you could say
he carries a bit of a beer belly,
which, to him, can be embarrassing,
but I couldn't imagine him any other way.

A grandfather who was much like a father
raised him with wisdom,
took him in and taught him what a man was
because he had never known one before.
This shaped him into the person he is today.

He is quiet,
and he keeps to himself,
Very motivated and hardworking,
he is a giving soul
with a caring heart.
This is how he sees himself.

Donna/Grandma/61

A crazy mother kept her away,
but she wishes she'd made more of an effort.
There were more talks they could've had,
and a better relationship could've been built.

She always wanted to be in food service,
which I find a little crazy,
but that is what she grew up to do,
managing restaurants.
And doing a damn good job at it.

At church, she feels less than
and lacking of education,
but at church, doesn't everyone feel
A little less than?
Judged by people whom think they're perfect.

Marrying her high school sweetheart
and growing together with him,
They built a life with each other,
and still, they are blossoming in love.
What a blessing it may be.

Caring, giving, a grandmother and wife,
she is a friend.
This is how she sees herself.
and every single word is true to her.

Lisa/Grandma/52

Self-care is something she wishes she'd started
younger,
taking care of her sweet mind and body,
eating healthier and working out more.
Now she's always reminding me how important it is.

As a young girl she was a dreamer,
you couldn't keep her feet on the ground.
She had dreams of being a dancer or writer,
although she is now neither.

The lack of self-care at a younger age,
has gifted her a few extra pounds.
This is where her concern lies,
in her fluff.

Failing has taught her much in life.
as it teaches us all.
She has learned, and she has grown
and that is to be admired.

She describes herself as giving, loving,
misunderstood, kind, and stubborn
(now I know where I get that last one from).

Betty/Great-Grandmother/83

Working for the government
under JFK,
why'd she ever leave?
She wishes she hadn't.

Dalmatians and sirens,
she wanted to be like her father,
big and brave,
fighting the flames.
He was a fireman.

Being such a small lady,
she finds it harder to lose weight,
She struggles with being confident in her own skin.

Meeting her mother-in-law has taught her much.
She was a wise woman
who knew many things,
things Betty would soon learn.

She sees herself as kind, loving, caring,
generous, and respectful.

Fred/Great-Grandfather/83

Circumstance arise,
but maybe he could've handled it better.
Making his wife quit her job,
that's something he shouldn't have done.

Trips overseas,
training to attack and being sent off on missions,
his dream was to be a navy pilot.

His temper is a spot of concern
that tends to embarrass him
if it gets out of hand.

High school brought him
the most valuable thing of all:
his wife-to-be.
They grew to love one another
despite their young age.
This would have a great impact on his life.

Compassionate, stubborn, respectful,
Laid-back, and helpful
are words he used to describe himself

Claire/22/Friend

Ignoring trembling hands
and tight chests,
she'd done it for too long,
stuffing emotions until she was overflowing,
much like this morning's coffee.
If only she'd sought help sooner.

Big dreams of the red carpet
and paparazzi,
a little girl standing in front of a mirror,
wearing lots of lip gloss
and a dress two sizes too big,
she was ambitious.
An actress is what she wanted to be

Doodles and little sketches,
she struggles to find her own kind of art
and, at times, find her artistic ability.
To be a bit embarrassing.

Having anxiety
has shaped her into the person she is.
It plays a huge role in her day-to-day life,
and learning to live with it
has posed a challenge,
but not one too big for her to accomplish.

She describes herself as
compassionate, articulate,
creative, loyal, and grounded.

Tom/68/Friend

The thing he most regrets
is what shaped him to love.
If only he could hold his mother's hand,
grip it tight,
Before saying one last final goodnight.

Standing up straight,
saluting, screams of "yes, sir."
Was his dream,
looking up to his daddy
That's all he wanted to be:
a soldier in uniform.
One boy can dream.

Doing his best to stay quiet,
constant hushing from his wife,
he is often embarrassed by his tone.
Occasionally, he is loud,
but not intentionally.
It's grown to be more of a habit.
Who knows? I don't notice.

Life is not the same
When you almost get your name
carved into a grave.
He lives to tell the story
of dying and not.

From that, he is mighty grateful,
a lover and proudly quieter than he once was.
He tells me he is a hungry person,
and yes for food.
That's not a figure of speech.
He is a nonviolent person.
This is how he sees himself.

Flipping through Becca's book of life,
she wishes she had been more trusting of herself.
Going with her gut wasn't a first response.
Maybe she always considered herself
to be more of a logical thinker.
A part of her regrets that
she never believed in her brilliant mind.

Like many little girls, she had dreams of being a teacher.
As a child, she would play pretend,
grading papers and creating sticker charts.
However, she did not grow up to be a teacher.

Instead, she ended up in full-time ministry,
walking out God's plan for her life.
This would have a great impact on her.
She was able to put what's most important to her first:
God.

I suppose you could say
she is a bit of a people pleaser.
and just like everyone else, she likes to be liked.
Others' thoughts about her cloud her mind.
She does her best to stand tall and love herself
despite the fiery comments others say
or the things she thinks they may think of her.

She lives a life filled with joy,
and her positive outlook on life bleeds into that.
Becca is a feeler, sensitive.

Her imagination
has always been able to fill a room.
She has never been afraid to take charge.
A leader, she is.

Eyde/60/Friend

The walk of faith is no easy one and
God never led her astray, but still,
she walked away.

When she was young,
she dreamed of being a teacher.
Playing school
was one of her favorite pastimes,
as well as mine.

She is worried about her weight,
concerned about her size,
even though no one else notices.
It's only in her mind.

Jesus has had the most impact on her life.
He loves her,
and she is glad she found her way back to him.
His unfailing love and blessings
have shown her what life is really about:
glorifying his name.

She describes herself as honest and a friend,
also empathetic and caring.
She is faithful and a servant.
I see her as all these things and more.

Jill isn't really a rock climber
or skydiver.
She wishes she was more adventurous
and luckily it's not too late.

Surgery on stuffed animals
that involved lots of band-aids,
she wanted to grow up
and save the lives of innocent pets.

Jill isn't fond of her pale legs.
Wearing shorts means putting them on display.
She still does it anyway
and this is an act of pure courage.

Her years spent in the Sunshine State
grew her in many ways.
She got a front-row seat to the palm trees
and diversity lacking back home.

Weird, silly, and skeptical,
curious, and a late bloomer,
all words she uses to describe herself.

Shannon/36/Friend

She went to be a teacher,
following her dreams,
before she realized it wasn't too thrilling.
Dropping out of college,
she could no longer decide what she wanted to pursue
This is something she regrets,too.

As I've said before, she wanted to be a teacher.
She threw on her mother's blouse and heels
before starting her long day of hard work
lining her stuffties up,
each one with a nametag.

She is self-conscious about her weight
even though her size is beautiful
and it doesn't define her.
When I see her, I think nothing of that
and everything of her kind heart.

Surrounded by like-minded people,
Christians like herself,
YWAM impacted her heavily.
She was a youth on a mission.

A listener, a daughter,
she issensitive, a reader,
and a procrastinator.
(She also has the cutest cats.)

Dan/22/Acquaintance

A big brother is someone who's forever present,
always there to protect and care.
His sister seemed to not want that.
In her efforts to be independent, she pushed him away,
and he wishes he'd tried harder to maintain a
relationship.

Spaceships built from cardboard boxes
and a cheese puff jar for a helmet,
he was ready to take off.
He'd always been fascinated with planets and stars
and whatever else space grips in its hand.

Piles of crumpled-up paper
and pencils snapping under the pressure of his hand,
He's too much a critic of himself,
and when it comes to his art,
he wants it to be just right.

Traveling to China at the young age of 19
to teach English.
He still remembers the cherry blossom trees
and the stale smell of the small apartment where he
stayed.

Dan describes himself as
reserved, adventurous, introverted,
diligent, and observant.

Hayley/32/Acquaintance

So what if they called her a try-hard?
She wishes she could have a re-do,
a second shot at college
to give it all she's got.
She isn't satisfied with her efforts.

Scuba dives, submarines, and all that it entailed,
she wanted to be under the sea
with sharks and jellyfish.
Marine biology, how hard could it be?

Mirrors are deceptive
And postpartum emotions are everywhere.
Heightened emotions and mean mirrors,
that's not good combo.

Interestingly enough, she didn't grow up in one place.
She was never grounded.
Moving from one country to the next,
she learned much about culture
at such a young age,
and for this, she is very grateful.

She is a lover of fun,
and damn, who isn't?
She says she is witty,
realistic, controlling,
and, much like me,
justice-minded.

Nikki/45/Stranger

There is no step-by-step
how-to for adulting
or a book to explain it all.
Life is a lot to manage,
and with only one shot,
it can be quite stressful.
So, yes, mistakes were made,
And there are more to come.

Oh, kids, how impressionable.
Anything you say may stick.
She learned how much of your life is shaped by
fundamentals.
She wanted to impact students the same way she was
impacted
in the classroom.

Tiny little hairs
coat her neck,
so scarfs are now everyday wear.
Such a tiny thing,
no one else notices,
but to her, it's embarrassing.

Monday night football, he spent it at the bar.
She was already home in bed.
A phone call saying. "We regret to inform you."
with a long pause.
Shots fired, which ended in the death of her husband.
Now she has a baby girl to raise alone.
She learned to survive on her own.

She describes herself as
resilient, faithful, compassionate,
spiritual, and loyal.

Ashley/32/Stranger

She should've just paused,
taken a moment for herself
to explore and venture
through different towns and pretty cities.

She grew to be
what she dreamt of becoming:
a teacher
striving to create an environment
for her kiddos to thrive.

After one of the most mind-boggling things,
pregnancy,
her body just didn't return to normal.
She couldn't seem to lose that bit of baby weight.
For her, it is a topic she doesn't love to discuss.

Traveling to teach
in a country many miles away,
she witnessed the excitement
of children for education
who were eager to learn,
much different from the America we know.

She is a thoughtful woman
with a joyous soul.
She is loyal and
observant.
This is how she sees herself.

Mary Beth/52/Stranger

Being young and immature
can be the cause of many mistakes.
At the time, she didn't see the importance of college.
Dropping out is something she still regrets.

Her love for children
grew her interest in the mission field.
From a young age,
her heart was set on making an impact,
and that, she did.

Public speaking, the main cause of death in many shy
people.
It's an area that she isn't exactly gifted in,
but that's okay.
She'll just avoid it at all costs

Much traveling
made her grow much in thanks,
more compassion, and mounds of love.

Loving, friendly, compassionate,
joyful, and grateful
are words she used to describe herself.

Larry/75/Stranger

Less of a regret
and more of wishing it wasn't reality:
the death of his beloved wife.
Still, he misses her every day.
Little things remind him of her laugh
or give him flashbacks of the way her perfume smelled
and how his name rolled off her tongue

Homegrown tomatoes from the garden,
plowing the fields, sowing seeds,
all that farming entails,
this is what he thought he'd grow to be.

His daily wardrobe must consist of a hat,
and despite his gray ponytail,
He is still self-conscious about being bald
I chuckled when he told me this;
It wasn't the answer I was expecting.

Many lessons taught and learned,
it seemed he grew just as much as his son.
Being a father blessed him with much in life,
like little grandbabies and proud father moments.

He describes himself as lucky, respectful, a grandfather
a worrier, and as healthy as a 75-year-old man can be.

Paul/36/Stranger

Now not to say no mistakes were made,
but he has no regrets.
Oh, what it must be like,
free of the bondage of regret.
He is not weighted down by a body full of
memories of a past he can never change.

Staticky hair and metal part
many of us know to be junk,
but he saw a vision so clear:
he would build a time machine.
As a little boy, he dreamed of being an inventor.

Biking, eh, not my thing,
but it seems to be his.
From Florida to California on the southern tier,
it was quite the adventure.
The most magnificent of views one has ever seen.

Paul describes himself as
Creative, loving, honest, fun and stubborn.

Amelia/32/Stranger

She lives a life with no regrets.
If only I could learn
to forgive and let go.
I too could live that life.

City to city,
Perhaps with a camera in hand,
many airplanes, and air bnb's
she chased this dream.
She grew to be only one of those things,
a photographer minus the world-traveling.
She still seems pretty happy to me.

When asked what makes her self-conscious,
she told me her hips,
but she couldn't give an explanation why,
and I didn't want to poke and pry,
so we left it at "I don't know why."

I'm not sure what this trauma looked like for her,
but I bet if I were taken back to that moment,
I would be able to smell the fear.
She is lucky she got away from the predator preying on her,
but how tragic it is to live with memories of what could have been.

She describes herself as
splintered, creative, intuitive, sensitive,
and determined.

Acknowledgements

To my beautiful mess of a family who stood behind me every step of the way. A special thanks to my mom who takes on the role of my best friend, shares with me the fondest memories and never allows me to forget how loved I am.

To the community of people that cheered me on and gave me much needed encouragement through this long process.

To every poet I fell in love with, thank you. Your words kept me going and inspired me to never give up on this dream.

To my dear friends, thank you for letting me read my work to you. I know poetry isn't your thing, but you loved me enough to listen.

And to you my reader. Thank you for reading these heavy pages and continuing to venture on. I dedicate this book to you. May you now know you aren't alone.

If you or someone you know is battling with suicidal thoughts or actions don't hesitate to reach out. Asking for help doesn't make you weak, it makes you brave.

National suicide prevention hotline 1-800-273-8255

Ten facts about suicide

1. Nearly 800,000 people die by suicide around the world each year

2. Suicide is the 2nd leading cause of death in ages 15 to 24

3. There is estimated to be one suicide for every 25 suicide attempts

4. Only half of all Americans battling depression receive help

5. Females are more likely than males to experience suicidal thoughts

6. Depression effects 20-25% of Americans ages 18+ in one year

7. 80-90% of people who seek treatment for depression are successfully helped through medication or therapy

8. An estimated quarter of a million people survive suicide attempts each year

9. In the US there is one death by suicide every 12 minutes

10. Lesbian, gay, and bisexual kids are 3x more likely than a straight kids to attempt suicide at some point in there life

Made in the USA
Columbia, SC
18 January 2020

86913705R00059